COLLECTIONS

A Harcourt Reading / Language Arts Program

*Set sail for
surprise
and adventure.*

SET SAIL

SENIOR AUTHORS
Roger C. Farr • Dorothy S. Strickland • Isabel L. Beck

AUTHORS
Richard F. Abrahamson • Alma Flor Ada • Bernice E. Cullinan • Margaret McKeown • Nancy Roser
Patricia Smith • Judy Wallis • Junko Yokota • Hallie Kay Yopp

SENIOR CONSULTANT
Asa G. Hilliard III

CONSULTANTS
Karen S. Kutiper • David A. Monti • Angelina Olivares

Harcourt

Orlando   Boston   Dallas   Chicago   San Diego

Visit *The Learning Site!*

www.harcourtschool.com

Dear Reader,

   Set Sail for the adventures that are waiting for you in this book! Like some of the characters in the stories, you may be surprised by what you find. Whether you explore your own backyard or go far away, there is always something new to learn.

   Now turn the page so your adventures can begin!

Sincerely,

The Authors

The Authors

THEME
Going Places

CONTENTS

THEME
Going Places

6

Reader's Choice

Little Fox Goes to the End of the World

by Ann Tompert
illustrated by John Wallner

Little Fox tells her mother about everything she will see and do on a trip to the end of the world.

FROM THE LIBRARY

Peeping
and Sleeping

by Fran Manushkin
illustrated by Jennifer Plecas

Barry and his dad go outside to find
out what is making a peeping noise.

FROM THE LIBRARY

The Big Dipper

by Franklyn M. Branley
illustrated by Molly Coxe

Learn how to find the Big
Dipper, the Little Dipper, and the
North Star in this fact-filled book!

FROM THE LIBRARY

The Story of a Blue

by Tomek Bogacki

Bird

A little blue bird was born
in the nest of a big tree. He
grew fast.

"Why don't you go and learn how to fly with your brother and sister? Don't you wonder what is out there?" his mother asked. "Oh, yes. But I am still a little bit afraid," the blue bird answered.

So while the other birds tested their wings the little blue bird sat in the nest, watching.

At night he couldn't sleep,
imagining what might be
out there beyond the trees.

"Mama, Mama, what is out
there?" he asked.
"Nothing," she said. "Now
go to sleep."

Nothing? he wondered . . .
And he couldn't stop
thinking about it.

16

17

The next morning the little
blue bird was gone, and
everyone wondered what
had happened.

"Nothing, nothing, where
is this nothing?" the little
blue bird thought as he
walked away from his nest
in the big tree.

"Is nothing high, or is
nothing low?
Is nothing here, or is
nothing there?
What does nothing
look like?"

There was no one to ask,
so he kept on going.

21

He came upon a pool of
blue water. It looked like
nothing he had ever seen
before, but he didn't know
if this was the nothing he
was looking for.

"What are you looking for?"
someone asked him.

"Nothing," he answered,
surprised.
"Oh! Come with me," said
the green bird.

And the blue bird joined
him.

24

Suddenly a flock of colorful
birds came flying by.

"What are you looking for?"
they asked.

"Nothing," the green bird
answered.

"Oh! Come with us,"
they called.

And the green bird spread
his wings and flew up.

25.

And the little blue bird
forgot that he was afraid
of flying. He, too, spread
his wings and flew up to
join them.

And they flew high, and
they flew low. They flew
here, and they flew there.

"How wonderful it is to fly,"
the little blue bird thought.

"Where have you been? What have you seen?" asked his brother and sister when the blue bird came back home.

"What happened to make you fly so well?" asked his mother.

"Nothing," said the blue bird, happily fluttering his wings.

"Tell us, tell us all about it," said his brother and sister.

"Come with me!" said the blue bird.

And they flew high, and they flew low.
They flew here, and they flew there.
They flew everywhere . . . all together.

Think About It

1. What was the little blue bird looking for? What did he find?

2. Tell about the first time you tried to do something. What did you do? How did you feel?

3. Why was it easier for the little blue bird to fly with his new friends?

31

Meet the Author/Illustrator

Tomek Bogacki

Tomek Bogacki grew up in his grandparents' big house near a river in Poland. He rode his bike to the meadows at the edge of town. He also drew, painted, and wrote stories.

Now Tomek Bogacki illustrates and writes children's books. Children all over the world have enjoyed them, so he keeps making new ones.

Tomek Bogacki

Visit *The Learning Site!*
www.harcourtschool.com

If you could Fly...

Imagine what it would be like to fly like a bird. Where would you go? What do you think you could see from the air? Draw a picture of the places you would like to see.

34

Write about what you drew.

Share your work with your classmates.

Hang your work around the classroom.

I flew over a park.
I saw lots of trees.
I saw a man walking his dog.

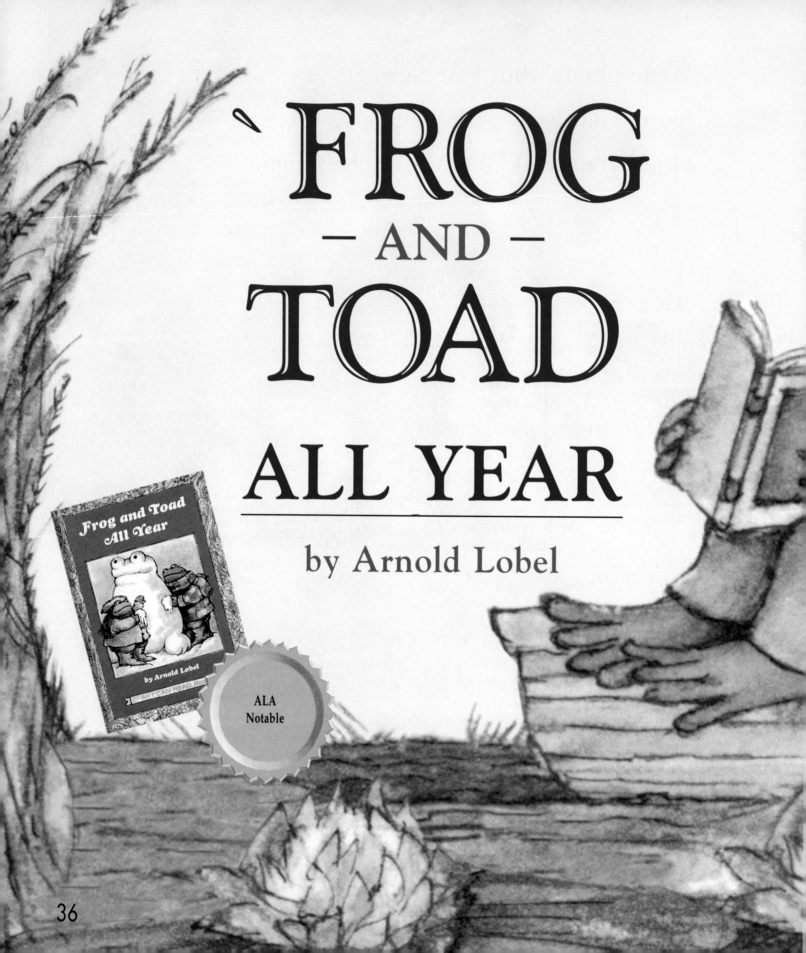

`FROG
– AND –
TOAD
ALL YEAR

by Arnold Lobel

ALA
Notable

THE CORNER

Frog and Toad

were caught in the rain.

They ran to Frog's house.

"I am all wet," said Toad.

"The day is spoiled."

"Have some tea and cake,"

said Frog. "The rain will stop.

If you stand near the stove,

your clothes will soon be dry.

I will tell you a story

while we are waiting," said Frog.

"Oh good," said Toad.

"When I was small,

not much bigger

than a pollywog," said Frog,

"my father said to me,

'Son, this is a cold, gray day

but spring

is just around the corner.'

I wanted spring to come.

I went out

to find that corner.

I walked down a path in the woods

until I came to a corner.

I went around the corner

to see if spring

was on the other side."

"And was it?" asked Toad.

"No," said Frog.

"There was only a pine tree,
three pebbles
and some dry grass.

I walked

in the meadow.

Soon I came to

another corner.

I went around the corner

to see if spring was there."

"Did you find it?" asked Toad.

"No," said Frog.
"There was only
an old worm
asleep on a
tree stump."

"I walked along the river
until I came to
another corner.
I went around the corner
to look for spring."
"Was it there?" asked Toad.

"No," said Frog.
"There was only
some wet mud
and a lizard who was chasing
his tail."
"You must have been tired,"
said Toad.
"I was tired," said Frog,
"and it started
to rain."

"I went back home.

When I got there," said Frog,

"I found another corner.

It was the corner of my house."

"Did you go around it?"
asked Toad.

"I went around that corner, too,"
said Frog.

"What did you see?"
asked Toad.

"I saw the sun coming out,"
said Frog. "I saw birds
sitting and singing in a tree.
I saw my mother and father
working in their garden.
I saw flowers in the garden."

"You found it!" cried Toad.

"Yes," said Frog.

"I was very happy.

I had found the corner

that spring was just around."

"Look, Frog," said Toad.

"You were right.

The rain has stopped."

Frog and Toad hurried outside.

They ran around the corner
of Frog's house
to make sure
that spring had come again.

Think About It

1 What did you like most about
this story? Tell why.

2 Tell what Frog does to find
spring. Then tell what Frog and
Toad do together to find it.

3 How does Frog's story help
Toad feel better?

ABOUT THE AUTHOR/ILLUSTRATOR

ARNOLD LOBEL

Arnold Lobel was both a writer and an illustrator of books for children. Frog and Toad are two of the many wonderful characters he created. He got the idea to write about frogs and toads while sitting on his front porch. He thought about frogs and toads, which look alike but are very different. Then he began writing about the characters we know today.

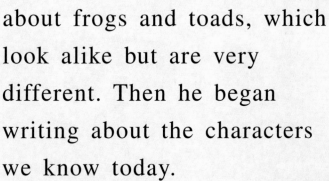

 Visit *The Learning Site!* www.harcourtschool.com

Frogs in Trees?

by Mark Warner

What do you think of when you think of frogs? Things that hop, right? Well how about things that *climb?* Some frogs climb bushes and trees. These frogs are called *tree frogs.*

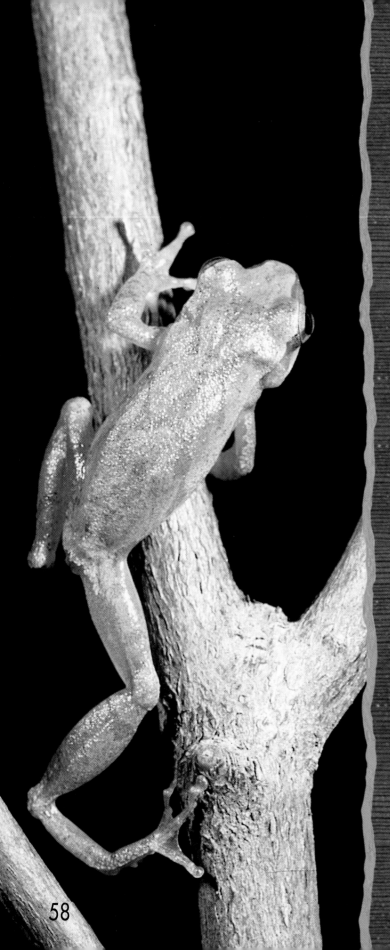

The tree frogs climb trees to look for food. The big eyes on top of their heads make it easy for them to see insects they want to eat. The big eyes also help the tree frogs see bigger animals that might want to eat them!

◄ Tree frogs have sticky pads on the tips of their toes. These pads help them hold on to trees as they climb.

58

Most tree frogs are small. ▶
Being small makes it easier
to climb trees. This full-grown
tree frog can easily fit on a
person's thumb.

Tree frogs are good at ▶
hiding. Some even change
color to help them hide.
This gray tree frog blends in
with the tree bark. Can you
see the frog?

Teacher Read-Aloud

RESPONSE ACTIVITY

JUMP AND MEASURE

Frogs and toads jump from place to place. One kind of frog can jump more than 17 feet in one jump!

See how far you can jump.

YOU WILL NEED:

masking tape, yarn, and scissors

1 Work in a group of three. Mark a starting line with masking tape.

2 From the starting line, jump as far as you can. Stand still where you land.

3 One person holds the end of the yarn at the starting line. The other walks to where the jumper landed and cuts the yarn.

4 Write your name on a piece of tape. Tape it to your yarn. Do this for each group member.

Compare the pieces of yarn. Put them in order from shortest to longest. Who jumped the farthest?

The P

uddle

by David McPhail

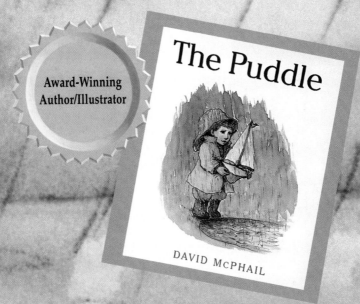

Award-Winning
Author/Illustrator

The Puddle

DAVID McPHAIL

It was a rainy day.

I asked my mom if I
could go out and sail
my boat in the puddles.
She said, "Okay, but *you*
stay out of the puddles."

I got dressed in my rain boots and coat, and went to sail my boat in the largest puddle I could find.

A frog came along and
sat down beside me.
"Nice boat," he said.

Then he jumped onto my boat and
sailed away. "Come back!" I called,
but he wouldn't listen.

A turtle floated by.

"Teatime," said the turtle. "Care to join me?"

"I can't," I said. "I need to get my boat back.

Besides, I'm not allowed to go in puddles."

But the frog steered my boat right into the
turtle. CRASH!
The frog laughed. He thought it was funny.

The turtle didn't think it was funny at all.
She was angry.

Then an alligator offered to help.
"Want me to get your boat back
for you?" he asked.
"Really? That would be *great*!" I said.

So the alligator swam out to take
my boat away from the frog.
He did.

But the boat looked different
than it did before.
"Sorry," he said.
"Don't worry about it,"
I told him.

Next, a pig wanted
to swim in the puddle.

He took a running start,
jumped in, and splashed me.
"My mom's not gonna like this!"
I yelled to the pig.

Before long, a thirsty
elephant showed up.

She drank . . .
and drank . . .

. . . until the puddle
was nearly gone.

The other animals were
upset with the elephant.
"Put back the water!"
they shouted.

So she did.

She left, and when the sun
started to come out, the
other animals left, too.

Then the sun dried up
the rest of the puddle.
I took my boat home.

When I got there, my mom had a hot
bath waiting for me.
"Can I bring my boat?" I asked her.
"Of course," she said.

And I did.

Think About It

1 What is your favorite part of the story? Tell why.

2 What happens when the boy tries to sail his boat in the puddle?

3 How does the author mix the real and the make-believe parts of the story?

Meet the Author/Illustrator

David McPhail

David McPhail grew up by the sea. He played in the woods and fields near his house. That is where he first got interested in animals. He likes to put animal characters in his stories.

He also likes to tell two stories in his books. He tells one in words and one in the illustrations. He believes that "each day is an adventure and each book is a new beginning."

David McPhail

Visit *The Learning Site!*
www.harcourtschool.com

83

Time to Play

Mama says to play outside.

Wish I had a bike to ride.

I'll fly to the moon instead.

Steer the rocket in my head.

I'll pretend to find a star

no one else has seen so far.

Then I'll name it after me—

Africa Lawanda Lee!

But for now I'll grab some chalk,

play hopscotch out on the walk.

by Nikki Grimes
illustrated by Floyd Cooper

Response
Activity

Places to Play

In "The Puddle," the boy went outside to play. Make a chart of games and activities to do indoors and outdoors.

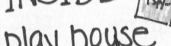

INSIDE
- play house
- read books
- do puzzles
- play school
- build with blocks

OUTSIDE
- jump rope
- ride bikes
- play soccer
- play tag
- play on the playground

1 Fold a sheet of paper in half.
Write INSIDE and OUTSIDE at the top.

2 Draw and write about your favorite things to do inside and outside.

Share your work with a group.
Talk about your ideas.

POPPLETON
Everyday

by Cynthia Rylant
illustrated by Mark Teague

THE NEW BED

One day Poppleton decided
to buy a new bed.
He liked his old bed.
But he'd had it since he was a boy.
Now he wanted a grown-up bed.

90

So Poppleton went to the bed store.

"Do you have a bed just right for a pig?"
he asked the saleslady.
"Hmmm," she said, looking Poppleton over.
"Right this way."

Poppleton followed the saleslady
to the biggest bed in the store.

It was vast! It was enormous!
"It's just my size!" said Poppleton.

He climbed on to test the bed.

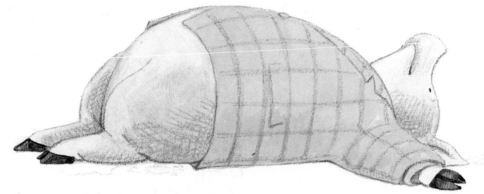

He lay on his back.

He lay on his side.

He lay with one leg over the edge.
He lay with both legs over the edge.

He lay on his head with his bottom in the air.

"How many different ways do you sleep?"
asked the saleslady.
"About twenty," said Poppleton.

"Do you have any books?" he asked.
The saleslady brought Poppleton a book.

Poppleton propped up some pillows
and read a few pages.
The saleslady looked at her watch.
"Do you want to buy the bed?"
she asked Poppleton.
"I don't know yet," said Poppleton.
"Do you have any crackers?"

The saleslady brought Poppleton
some crackers.
He got crumbs everywhere.
"Do you want the bed?"
asked the saleslady.

"I don't know yet," said Poppleton.
"Do you have a TV?"
The saleslady brought Poppleton a TV.
He watched a game show.

The saleslady checked her watch.
"Do you want the bed?"
she asked Poppleton.

"I don't know yet," said Poppleton.
"I have to check one more thing.
Do you have any bluebirds?"
"Pardon me?" said the saleslady.
"I always wake up to bluebirds,"
said Poppleton. "Do you have any?"

The saleslady went outside
and got three bluebirds to come in
and sing to Poppleton.
Poppleton lay with his eyes closed
and a big smile on his face.

"*Now* do you want the bed?"
asked the saleslady.

"Certainly!" said Poppleton.
And he picked up the book, the
crackers, the bluebirds, and the bed,
and happily went home.

Think About It

1. What does Poppleton do to test the bed before buying it?

2. Did you ever test something before making a decision? Tell about what you did.

3. What did you learn about Poppleton's character from reading this story?

CYNTHIA RYLANT

Cynthia Rylant grew up in the mountains of West Virginia. She spent a lot of time walking, playing, and thinking in the mountains. Now, she likes to send copies of her books to her family. "They are all so proud and happy to receive them," says Cynthia. "It's nice to have a job people are so enthusiastic about!"

♡ Cynthia Rylant

Meet the Illustrator

MARK TEAGUE

Mark Teague was working in a bookstore in New York City when he remembered how much he liked picture books as a child. He thought about how much he enjoyed writing and illustrating his own stories when he was a boy. He began writing and illustrating children's books and has illustrated more than 15 of them.

Mark Teague

Visit *The Learning Site!*
www.harcourtschool.com

RESPONSE ACTIVITY

TIME FOR BED

What do you do to get ready for bed?
Show the order of the things you do at bedtime.

YOU WILL NEED:

• 5 or 6 blank cards   • tape   • markers or crayons

1 Write your name on one card.

2 Think about what a person does at bedtime. On another card, write the first thing. Draw a picture.

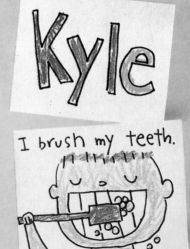

110

3 Use a different card for each thing you add.

4 Put your cards in order, with your name on top. Tape the cards together.

5 Share your list with others. Did you put the things in the same order or a different order?

Moon

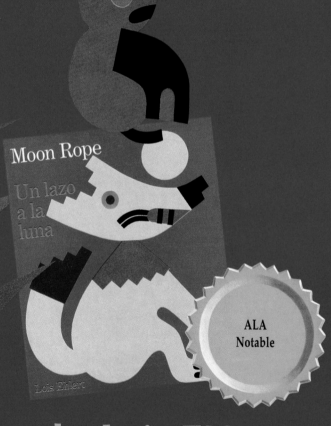

Moon Rope

Un lazo a la luna

Lois Ehlert

ALA
Notable

by Lois Ehlert

Rope

Mole was taking a break
from digging for worms
when Fox came by.

"Mole," he said, "if you
could have anything in the
world, what would it be?"

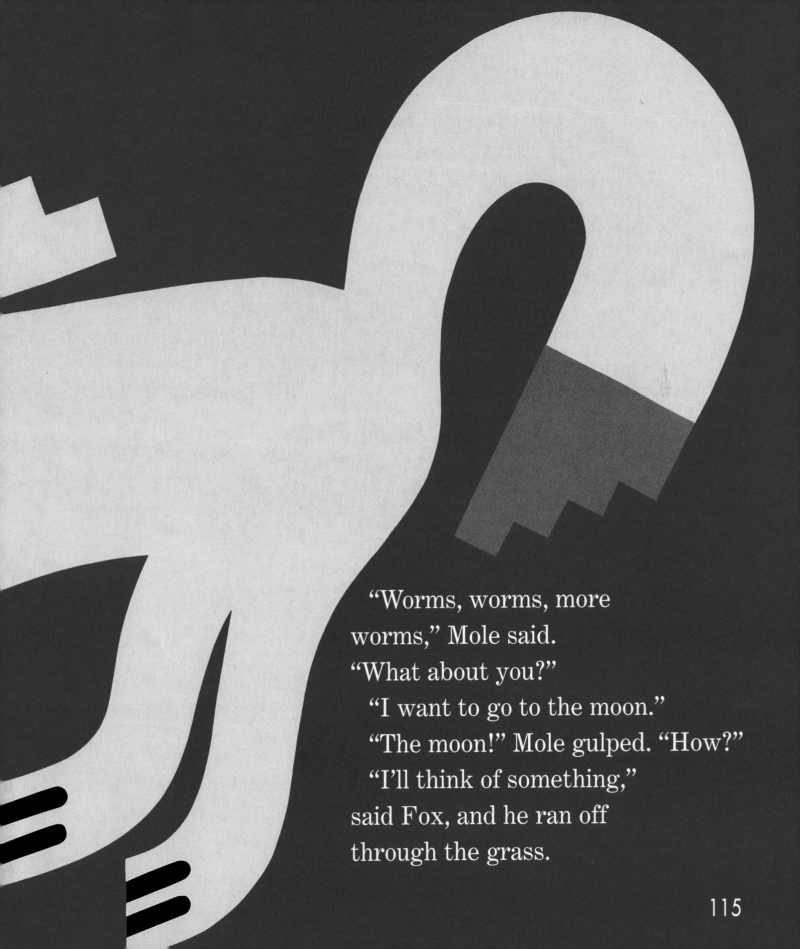

"Worms, worms, more
worms," Mole said.
"What about you?"
   "I want to go to the moon."
   "The moon!" Mole gulped. "How?"
   "I'll think of something,"
said Fox, and he ran off
through the grass.

Fox liked running through the grass. It tickled
his fur, and that gave him an idea. Why not make
a rope of grass? With a loop at one end, he could
hitch it to the tip of the moon and climb up.

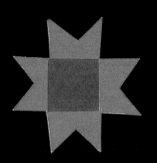

Fox ran back.

"Mole! I've got it!
Both of us can climb to
the moon on my rope."

Mole blinked. "Both of us?"

"There are big worms up there,"
said Fox. "Huge."

Mole's stomach growled. He'd go.

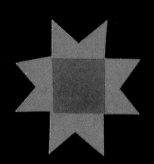

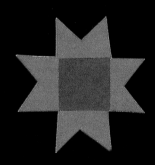

Mole and Fox braided grass into a long rope
and waited for a crescent moon to appear.
Then Fox twirled the rope high over his head.

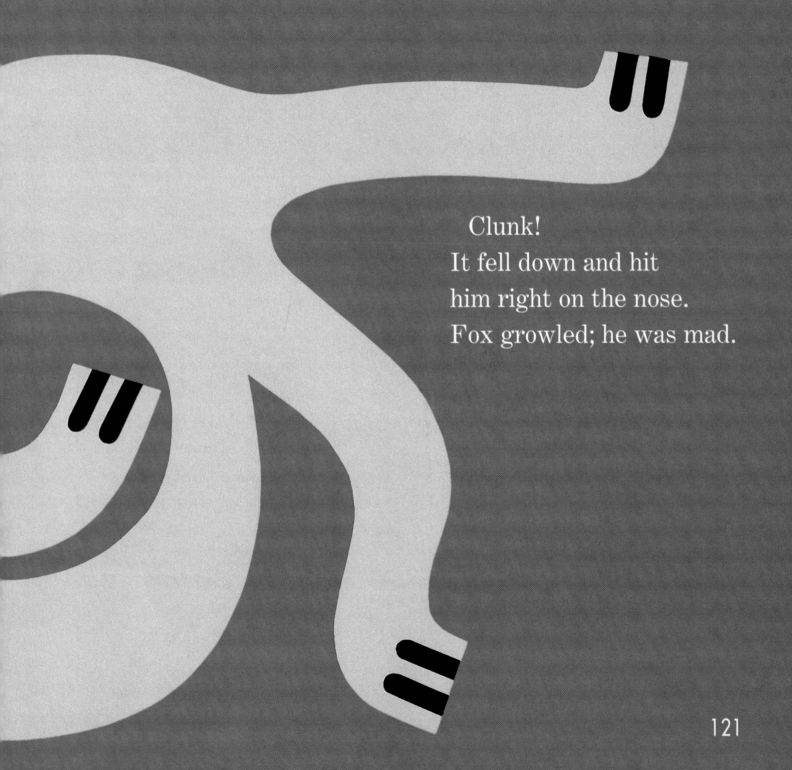

Clunk!
It fell down and hit
him right on the nose.
Fox growled; he was mad.

"Maybe the birds would
carry our rope," said Mole.
But the birds didn't want to
go to the moon.
 "Just hitch this rope to the
tip," said Fox. "We'll do the rest."

So the birds took the rope
in their beaks and flew up,
up, up into the sky. Mole
and Fox waited.

When they returned, the birds said,
"Your rope is ready." Fox started
climbing, paw over paw, eager
to be first on the moon.
Mole followed,
claw over claw.

Fox kept his eyes on the moon.
But not Mole. He kept glancing
back to earth. Suddenly Mole's
claws slipped. He fell through
the air, down, down, down . . .

Ploomph!
Mole landed on a bird.
They had been following the
two climbers. Mole hung on
tightly as he was carried back
home. He hoped to land unnoticed.

But all the creatures were watching. They laughed at Mole.

"Maybe you didn't slip," said Snake. "Maybe you let go on purpose so you could come back home."

131

Mole was upset by all the
fuss. He ran away and dug a
deep tunnel. He stayed there
for a long, long time.

To this day Mole prefers to come out after dark, moving quietly in the moonlight, avoiding the other creatures. And he never ever listens to a fox.

But what about Fox?
Did he make it to the moon?
The birds say that on a clear night they can
see him in the full moon, looking down on
earth. Mole says he hasn't seen him.
Have you?

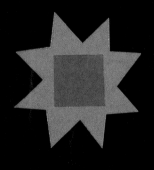

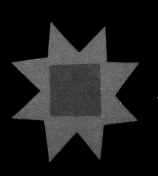
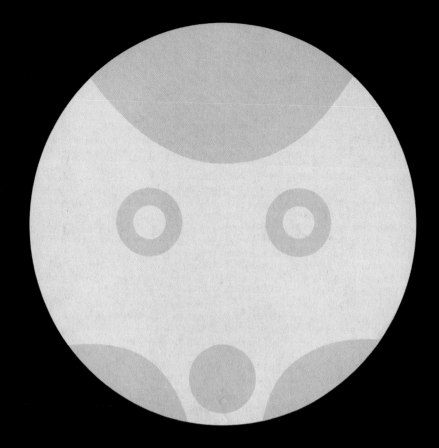

Think About It

1 Tell whether you think Fox's idea worked. Use story events to back up your ideas.

2 Have you ever had an idea and tried to make or build something? What happened?

3 This folktale tells why something in nature is the way it is. What does this tale explain?

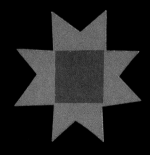

Lais Ehlert

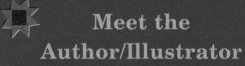

Lois Ehlert

When she was a girl, Lois Ehlert used scraps of wood and cloth to make things. Later, she went to art school and became an illustrator. She looked at art from Peru— cloth, jewelry, pottery, and sculpture— to create the pictures for *Moon Rope*, a folktale from Peru.

 Visit *The Learning Site!*
www.harcourtschool.com

Collage Animals

Make collage animals and tell a story about them.

You will need:

ribbons

scissors

cloth scraps

construction paper

feathers

buttons

glitter

markers

crayons

glue

■ Choose an animal that you like.

■ Use different materials to make that animal.

■ Try a few different things before you glue the materials.

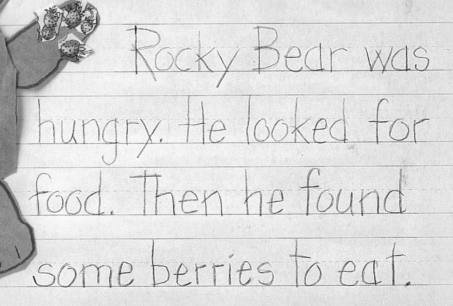

Rocky Bear was hungry. He looked for food. Then he found some berries to eat.

■ When you finish your animal collage, write a story about your animal.

■ Then share your story with a group.

The Big Big Sea

by Martin Waddell
illustrated by Jennifer Eachus

Mama said, "Let's go!"
So we went . . .

out of the house
and into the dark
and I saw . . .
THE MOON.

We went over the field
and under the fence
and I saw
the sea in the moonlight,
waiting for me.

And I ran
and Mama ran.
We ran and we ran,
straight through the puddles
and out to the sea!

I went right in
to the shiny bit.
There was only me
in the big big sea.

I splashed
and I laughed
and Mama came after me
and we paddled
out deep in the water.

We got all wet.

Then we walked
a bit more
by the edge of the sea
and our feet
made big holes
in the sand.

Far far away,
right around the bay,
were the town
and the lights
and the mountains.
We felt very small,
Mama and me.

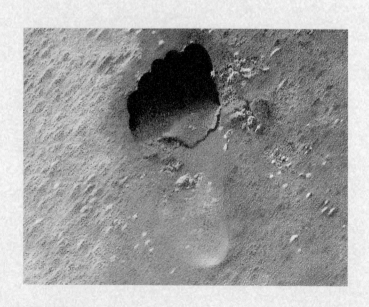

We didn't go to the town.
We just stayed for a while
by the sea.

And Mama said to me,
"Remember this time.
It's the way life should be."

I got cold
and Mama carried me
all the way back.

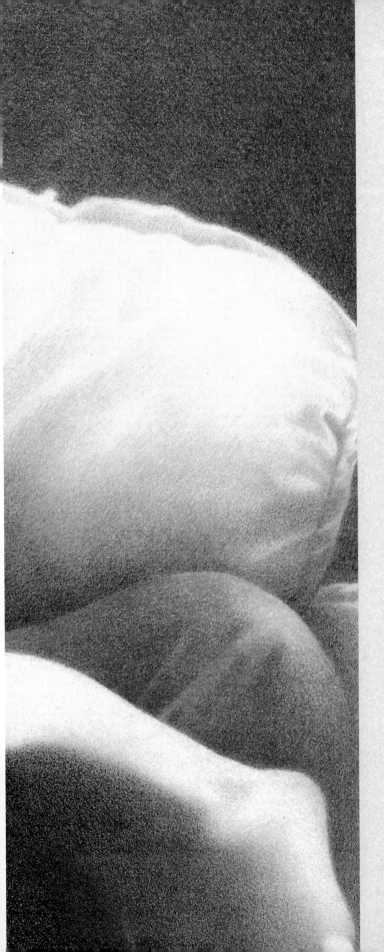

We sat by the fire,
Mama and me,
and ate hot buttered toast
and I went to sleep
on her knee.

I'll always remember
just Mama and me
and the night
that we walked
by the big big sea.

Think About It

1 What will the girl
remember about the night
in the story?

2 Why do you think the
author made the girl's
mother tell her to
"remember this time"?

3 Tell about a special time
that you will always
remember.

THE FISH THAT GOES FISHING

FROM <u>FISH DO THE STRANGEST THINGS</u>
by Leonora and Arthur Hornblow

People catch many strange fish.
But one of the strangest fish of all
does her own fishing.
She lives down deep in the dark sea.
She is called the deep-sea angler.
The deep-sea angler has
her own fishing rod.
It grows out of the top of
her head and hangs in
front of her mouth.
The tip of her rod shines in
the deep dark water.

This tip is the bait on her fishing rod. Hungry fish see her bait. They think it is something to eat. A hungry fish will swim toward the shiny bait.

The angler opens her wide mouth. The fish swims closer and closer. He swims right at the bait. Then the angler closes her mouth. Snap! That's the end of that fish.

illustrated by Bernie Knox

In the Deep Blue Sea

Have you ever been to the ocean? What do you know about the big, big sea? What animals live there? Make a mural about life in the sea.

fish

eel

octopus

shark

sea stars

1. Make a list of animals that live in the ocean.

2. Read about those animals.

3. Decide what animals to show and where to draw them.

4. Put the mural in the hallway for others to see.

whale

seahorse

sting ray

eel

fish

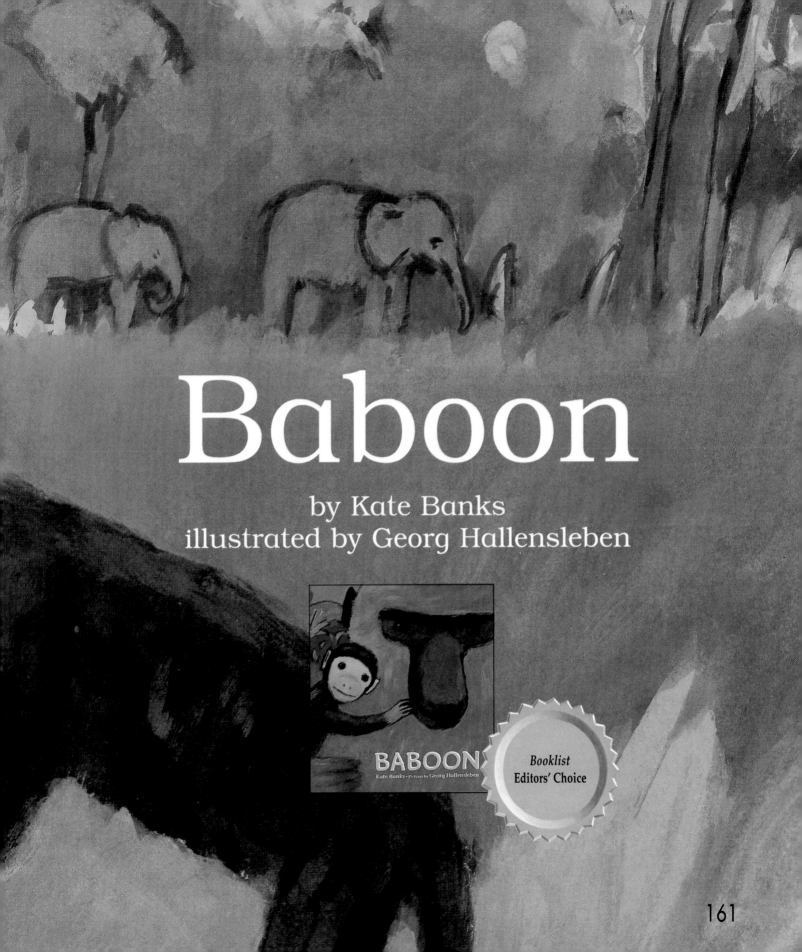

Baboon

by Kate Banks
illustrated by Georg Hallensleben

BABOON
Kate Banks · Pictures by Georg Hallensleben

Booklist
Editors' Choice

Baboon opened his sleepy eyes.
Ahead was the great forest.
"Look," said his mother. "That is
the world."
Baboon slid from his mother's back.
"So, the world is green," he said.
"Some of it," said his mother. And
she led Baboon among the tall trees.

A turtle sat in the middle of the road.
Its eyes were closed and it barely moved.
Baboon watched and waited for the turtle
to pass. He waited a long time.
"The world is slow," he said.
"It can be," said his mother.

When the turtle had passed, Baboon followed
his mother.
At the edge of the great forest, a fire burned
in the bush.
Baboon moved close to the fire.
Soon he could feel its heat.
Baboon leaped backward.
"The world is hot!" he said.
"Not always," said his mother.

She led Baboon to a small lake.
A crocodile lay on the sandy bank.
It opened its mouth wide.
"Careful," said Baboon's mother.
"The crocodile might eat you."
Baboon did not want to be eaten.
So he ran into the bush.
"The world is hungry," he said.
"Sometimes you are hungry, too,"
said his mother.

169

Soon the elephants came, four by four.
They thundered loud and shook the ground.
A gazelle passed. He was not slow like the
turtle, but quick and fast.

171

A rhinoceros darted out of the bushes.
He grunted at Baboon. Baboon was afraid.
"He will not hurt you," said his mother.

Baboon took his mother's hand, and they
started across a field.
Baboon hid in the tall grass.
His mother hid, too. When they found each
other, they lay down, side by side.
"The world is soft," said Baboon. And he
was happy.

Baboon stretched and rolled over.
A bird flew by. A cloud passed
overhead. And Baboon fell asleep.
When he awoke, the sun was going down.
Baboon watched it disappear behind the trees.
"Come along," said his mother. And they
walked on.

Baboon followed his mother up
a tree.
Across from him sat a monkey.
He was like Baboon.
"Is he the world, too?" asked Baboon.
"He is," said his mother. "Just as
you are."
Baboon watched quietly.
Then he followed his mother down
the tree.

179

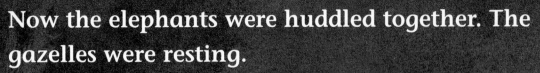

Now the elephants were huddled together. The gazelles were resting.
There was no more fire and the light was gone from the sky.
Baboon climbed onto his mother's back.
"The world is dark," he said.
"Sometimes," whispered his mother, carrying him home.

Baboon looked around.

He blinked.

Everything was black as far as he could see.

He laid his head against his mother's soft neck.

"The world is big," he said.

"Yes," said his mother softly. "The world is big."

Think About It

1 How did Baboon's mother help him learn about the world?

2 Tell about a time when you learned something new about a place you visited.

3 What clues in the story let you know that it happens all in one day?

Meet the Author

Kate Banks

Kate Banks and her four-month-old son were looking at a picture of a mother baboon carrying her baby. That day, she began to think of the dialogue in "Baboon." Kate Banks likes watching, listening to, and being with children—she likes to write for them, too!

Kate Banks

Georg Hallensleben

Georg Hallensleben grew up in Germany. He loved riding his bike in the woods and drawing what he saw there. He used to bring his art supplies in a wooden case on his bike. He started drawing as a child and has never stopped!

G. Hallens

Visit *The Learning Site!*
www.harcourtschool.com

185

Piggyback

Mother bears give their cubs a ride when they get tired. Do your parents give you piggyback rides?

The water is not safe for baby grebes. Big fish eat little chicks. Mom and dad make great lifeboats.

Ride

This frog has two tadpoles on its back. They are on their way to a pool of water. The tadpoles will grow up there.

Young lemurs hold on tight when they go piggybacking. Lemur parents swing from trees with their babies on board!

Make a Mobile

The world is full of opposites. Baboon saw a **slow** turtle and a **fast** gazelle. He saw that the day was **light** and the night was **dark**.

You will need:
paper circles • string • hole punch • hanger

1 On one side of the circle, write one word and draw a picture.

2 On the other side, write the word that means the opposite and draw a picture for that word.

3 Punch a hole in the circle. Then tie a string to the circle. Tie the other end of the string to the hanger. Make your strings different lengths.

4 Then write pairs of sentences using the words on your mobile. Share your sentences with a group.

PLA

by Kim Jackson

NETS

Our world is a
planet named
Earth.

193

194

Nine planets move around the sun.

Our **sun** is not a planet. It is a **star**! Our sun gives us heat and light.

195

Planets close to the sun are very hot.

Planets far from the sun are very cold.

A planet named **Mercury** is closest to the sun. Mercury is very hot!

A planet named **Venus** looks bright. From Earth, Venus looks bright, like a star!

A planet
named **Mars**
is red.
Mars has
two moons!

A planet named **Jupiter** is very big. Jupiter is the biggest planet.

A planet
named **Saturn**
has rings.

The rings are
made of
ice and **rock**.

A planet
named **Uranus**
also has rings.
Uranus has rings
and moons!

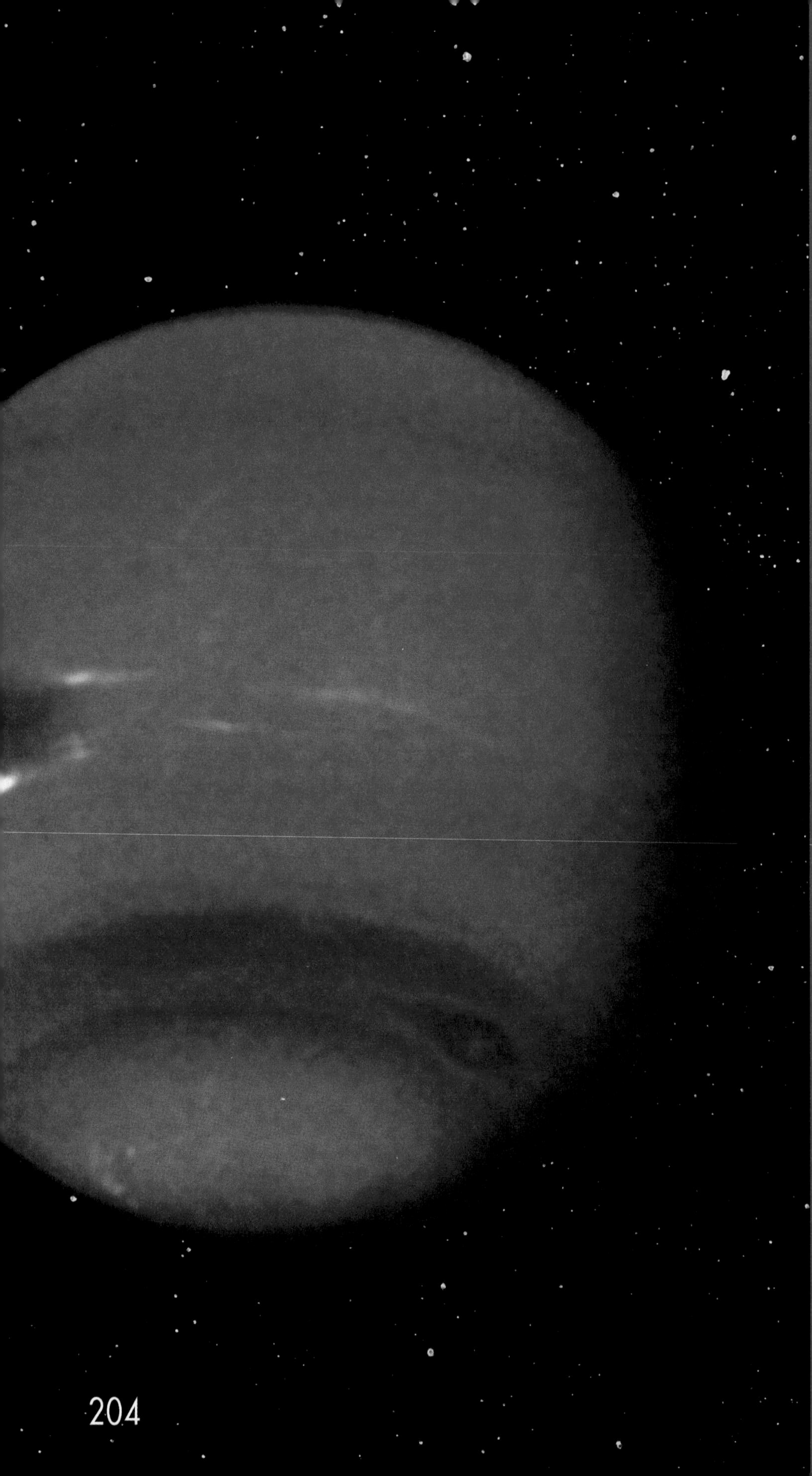

A planet
named
Neptune
is far away.
Neptune is
almost too far
for us to see.

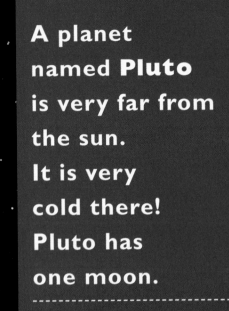

A planet
named **Pluto**
is very far from
the sun.
It is very
cold there!
Pluto has
one moon.

Our planet **Earth** is just right for us.
Maybe someday we will visit the other
planets. Which planet would you visit?

Think About It

1. What did you learn about our solar system?

2. Which planet would you like to visit? Tell why.

3. How did the photographs help you understand what you read?

About the Photographs

The *Voyager*
spacecraft

The Hubble
telescope

Voyager took many
of the pictures in "Planets." This
spacecraft was sent into space on a
rocket. First it took pictures of Earth.
Then it flew far from home. It took
pictures of planets, stars, and other
space objects.

Now the Hubble telescope is in space.
It takes pictures of objects in space that
are very far away. What do you think
this "eye in the sky" might see?

Visit *The Learning Site!*
www.harcourtschool.com

207

PLAY A
MEMORY
GAME

Share what you learned about planets. Make cards for a memory game.

YOU WILL NEED:
2 cards for each planet (18 in all)

Mercury

This planet is closest to the sun.

On one card, draw a picture of the planet. Write the name of the planet.

On another card, write a fact about the planet.

Now play a memory game with a partner. Place the cards face down.

Turn over two cards at a time. If you turn over a planet card and the fact that matches it, you keep both cards.

If the cards don't match, turn them over again.

Keep playing until you have matched every planet with a planet fact.

This planet has rings.

Saturn

Glossary

What Is a Glossary?

A glossary is like a small dictionary. This glossary is here to help you. You can look up a word and then read a sentence that uses that word. Some words have a picture to help you.

a·cross   They walked **across** the bridge.

a·fraid   My dog is **afraid** of thunder.

air   Birds and planes fly through the **air.**

ap·pear   After the sun sets, stars **appear** in the sky.

across

both   **Both** of your shoes are muddy.

boy   Every man was once a **boy**.

break   We'll take a **break** when we get tired.

brought   Kevin **brought** pictures from his trip to share with the class.

afraid

care   Would you **care** for some milk with your cookies?

caught   My dad got **caught** in traffic the other day.

211

cold

few

flew

clear   The sky looks very blue on **clear** days.

cold   If the weather gets **cold**, it may snow.

course   Of **course** you may come with us!

dif·fer·ent   Dogs and cats are **different** kinds of animals.

dis·ap·pear   The sun seemed to **disappear** behind the clouds.

edge   The baby pushed his peas to the **edge** of his dish.

few   We have only a **few** more pieces to add to the puzzle.

flew   The birds **flew** around all day.

ground The **ground** was covered with rocks and pebbles.

i·de·a It was George's **idea** to bring a snack for everyone.

joined Dan **joined** his friends at the lunch table.

knee I fell down and hurt my **knee.**

larg·est The blue whale is the **largest** living animal.

learn We **learn** a lot in school.

knee

lis·ten I like to **listen** to the radio.

mouth

mouth The hippopotamus has a very large **mouth.**

near I wish my grandparents lived **near** us.

planet

pic·tures We took lots of **pictures** at the party.

plan·et We live on the **planet** Earth.

quietly

qui·et·ly Our teacher wants us to walk **quietly** in the halls.

re·mem·ber My grandmother likes to **remember** stories from long ago.

rock·et   A **rocket** sends the shuttle into space.

shook   The ground **shook** when the train passed by.

son   Every boy is his parents' **son**.

space   I would like to be an astronaut and explore **space**.

space·craft   We could fly to Mars in a **spacecraft**.

straight   After my bath, I went **straight** to bed.

sure   Mindy counted the party favors to be **sure** she had enough for everyone.

rocket

son

work·ing   My whole family likes **working** in the garden.

Acknowledgments

For permission to reprint copyrighted material, grateful acknowledgment is made to the following sources:

The Blue Sky Press, an imprint of Scholastic Inc.: From "The New Bed" in *Poppleton Everyday* by Cynthia Rylant, illustrated by Mark Teague. Text copyright © 1998 by Cynthia Rylant; illustrations copyright © 1998 by Mark Teague.

Candlewick Press, Cambridge, MA: *The Big Big Sea* by Martin Waddell, illustrated by Jennifer Eachus. Text © 1994 by Martin Waddell; illustrations © 1994 by Jennifer Eachus.

Clarion Books, an imprint of Houghton Mifflin Company: Cover illustration by Jennifer Plecas from *Peeping and Sleeping* by Fran Manushkin. Illustration copyright © 1994 by Jennifer Plecas.

Farrar, Straus & Giroux, Inc.: *Baboon* by Kate Banks, illustrated by Georg Hallensleben. Text copyright © 1997 by Kate Banks; illustrations copyright © 1997 by Georg Hallensleben. *The Story of a Blue Bird* by Tomek Bogacki. Copyright © 1998 by Tomek Bogacki. *The Puddle* by David McPhail. Copyright © 1998 by David McPhail.

Nikki Grimes: "Time to Play" by Nikki Grimes. Text copyright © 1991 by Nikki Grimes.

Harcourt, Inc.: *Moon Rope* by Lois Ehlert. Copyright © 1992 by Lois Ehlert.

HarperCollins Publishers: Cover illustration by Molly Coxe from *The Big Dipper* by Franklyn M. Branley. Illustration copyright © 1991 by Molly Coxe. "The Corner" from *Frog and Toad All Year* by Arnold Lobel. Copyright © 1976 by Arnold Lobel.

Kirchoff/Wohlberg Inc., on behalf of Ann Tompert and John Wallner: Cover illustration by John Wallner from *Little Fox Goes to the End of the World* by Ann Tompert. Illustration copyright © 1976 by John Wallner.

National Wildlife Federation: "Piggyback Ride" from *Your Big Backyard* Magazine, February 1998. Text copyright 1998 by the National Wildlife Federation.

Random House Children's Books, a division of Random House, Inc.: From "The Fish That Goes Fishing" in *Fish Do the Strangest Things* by Leonora and Arthur Hornblow. Text copyright © 1966 by Random House, Inc.; text copyright renewed 1994 by Leonora Hornblow and Arthur Hornblow.

Scholastic Inc.: Illustration by Floyd Cooper from *Pass It On: African-American Poetry for Children,* selected by Wade Hudson. Illustration copyright © 1993 by Floyd Cooper. Published by arrangement with Just Us Books, Inc.

Troll Communications LLC: *Planets* by Kim Jackson. Text copyright © 1985 by Troll Communications.

Mark Warner: "Frogs in Trees?" by Mark Warner from *U. S. Kids, a Weekly Reader* Magazine.

Photo Credits

Key: (T)=top, (B)=bottom, (C)=center, (L)=left, (R)=right
Michael Campos Photography, 35; Ian Anderson, 54; Mark Warner, 56-59; Michael Campos Photography, 61; Carlo Ontal, 108; Michael Campos Photography, 111, 138, 139; courtesy, Walker Books, 156; Michael Campos Photography, 158, 159; Tony Dawson, 186(T); Don Enger/Animals Animals, 186(B); Michael Fogden/DRK Photo, 187(C); Wolfgang Kaehler, 187(B); Michael Campos Photography, 189, 208, 209
All other photos by Harcourt:
Rick Friedman/Black Star; Martin Benjamin/Black Star; Mark Derse/Black Star; David Levensen/Black Star; Anna Clopet/Black Star

Illustration Credits

Jui Ishida, Cover Art; Doug Bowles, 4-9; Tomek Bogacki, 10-35; George Kreif, 35; Arnold Lobel, 36-55, 60-61; David McPhail, 62-83; Floyd Cooper, 84-85; Tracy Sabin, 86-87, 110-111, 188-189, 208-209; Mark Teague, 88-111; Lois Ehlert, 112-139; Jennifer Eachus, 140-159; Georg Hallensleben, 160-185, 188-189